CHASING GUANO

The Discovery of a Penguin Supercolony

HELEN TAYLOR

TILBURY HOUSE PUBLISHERS

TILBURY HOUSE PUBLISHERS
an imprint of Cherry Lake Publishing Group
2395 South Huron Parkway, Suite 200 • Ann Arbor, MI 48104 • www.tilburyhouse.com

Library of Congress Cataloging-in-Publication Data

Names: Taylor, Helen, 1982- author.
Title: Chasing guano : the discovery of a penguin supercolony / Helen Taylor.
Description: [Ann Arbor, Michigan] : [Tilbury House Publishers,] [2024] | Series: How nature works | Audience: Ages 7-12 | Summary: "When a scientist came across a satellite image of the Antarctic's remote Danger Islands streaked with pink guano, she knew she was seeing evidence of a large, previously unnoticed colony of penguins. Join the team on an exploration as they discover one of the world's largest populations of Adélie penguins"-- Provided by publisher.
Identifiers: LCCN 2024011325 | ISBN 9781668944851 (hardcover)
Subjects: LCSH: Adélie penguin--Antarctica--Danger Islands--Juvenile literature. | Adélie penguin--Conservation--Antarctica--Danger Islands--Juvenile literature. | Adélie penguin--Antarctica--Antarctic Peninsula--Juvenile literature. | Adélie penguin--Conservation--Antarctica--Antarctic Peninsula--Juvenile literature. | Danger Islands (Antarctica)--Juvenile literature. | Antarctic Peninsula (Antarctica)--Juvenile literature. | Danger Islands Expedition (2015)--Juvenile literature.
Classification: LCC QL696.S473 T395 2024 | DDC 598.47--dc23/eng/20240430
LC record available at https://lccn.loc.gov/2024011325

Printed and bound in the United States

10 9 8 7 6 5 4 3 2 1

Photo Credits: © USGS/National Land Imaging Program, cover; © Gemma Clucas, cover, 2-3, 7, 18-19, 21, 28-29; © Rachel Herman, cover, 8-9,18-19; © Juliette Hannequinn, 1, 23, 29; © NOAA 3; © NASA 4, 5, 11, 13; © Heather Lynch, 6-7, 33, 36; ©2024, Ron Naveen/OCEANITES, 6; © Angus Henderson, 7; © Casey Youngflesh, 9, 10-11, 12, 12-13, 14-15, 20, 25, 26-27, 30-31; © Thomas Sayre-McCord, 26, 32-33; © Bob Zuur, 15; © Philip McDowall, 16-17; © Alex Borowicz, 17, 20-21, 31, 39, 38-39; © Farjana.rahman/Shutterstock, 19; © Michael Polito, 22-23, 22, 27, 29, 34-35; © Christian Aslund/Greenpeace, 23; © Tom Hart, 24-25, 27; © The Pew Charitable Trusts, 37

The Danger Islands, off the tip of the Antarctic Peninsula, are teeming with penguins. Unseen. Uncounted. Unprotected. Hidden in plain sight, but not for long. . . .

Larsen
Ice Shelf

Antarctic
Peninsula

Wilkins
Ice Shelf

Their *poop* is
visible from space!

In satellite photos taken 438
miles above Earth, the Danger
Islands are streaked with pink.

Satellites in the Landsat
program photograph Earth's
surface year-round.

Heather, an American scientist who uses satellite images to study Antarctic wildlife from afar, knows penguin poop—guano—when she sees it.

To complement her remote monitoring work, Heather also conducts field research in Antarctica.

Based on its color, she knows
what these birds like to eat too:
pink krill.

Antarctic krill

Penguins hunt at sea, but nest on land.

For scientists like Heather, penguins are a link between two worlds. A window onto a changing ecosystem.

WHY PENGUINS?

Penguins nest on shore, eat at sea, and dodge predators in both places. That makes penguins very interesting to ecologists and climate researchers who want to understand how environmental changes are affecting life along Antarctica's coastline. Few animals are as busy both above and below the water's surface. When penguins come ashore to rebuild their nests each year, scientists conduct counts to track how colonies are growing, shrinking, or moving over time. Changes seen at the penguin colony level can alert researchers to larger issues brewing—issues that could throw the whole ecosystem off balance.

The Antarctic Peninsula is warming and many of its penguin colonies are shrinking. The race is on to understand why—because trouble at the bottom of the world could ripple far and wide.

ALL ABOUT SEA ICE

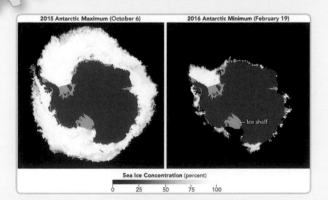

2015 Antarctic Maximum (October 6)   2016 Antarctic Minimum (February 19)

— Ice shelf

Sea Ice Concentration (percent)

0   25   50   75   100

Antarctica is surrounded by a ring of frozen seawater known as sea ice that grows and shrinks each year. In the winter, so much of the surrounding ocean freezes that Antarctica nearly doubles in size! Unlike the freshwater ice sheets covering the continent itself, which are up to three miles deep, sea ice is salty and only about three feet thick. When the weather warms up each summer, most of it melts.

Creatures big and small depend on sea ice—and its freeze-thaw cycle—for habitat and food. Each year, as temperatures rise and the sea ice retreats, phytoplankton (floating microalgae) blooms in the water. Krill eat those phytoplankton. Bigger animals follow the krill. Some, like humpback whales, travel thousands of miles for the feast.

But when the ice melts early, or in a different spot than usual, it's like moving a party without telling the guests. Some hungry partygoers have trouble adjusting and miss out, with potentially dire consequences.

Heather has studied Antarctic penguins for years, but the Danger Islands had escaped her attention until now. They're tiny. And, surrounded by sea ice all year, they're particularly difficult to reach. Dangerous, even. But the sight of all that guano means it's time for a closer look.

How big is this colony?

How long has it been there?

Is it shrinking too?

OUR CHANGING CLIMATE

HOW NATURE WORKS

While Antarctica may seem far away, what happens there impacts us all. Its ice sheets affect wind patterns and weather around the world. The Southern Ocean's frigid waters are a major driver of global ocean circulation. We even count on Antarctica's bright white ice to reflect some of the sun's rays back into space, helping regulate our air and ocean temperatures. But Earth's climate is changing, which means those crucial processes are subject to change too. As our poles warm up, ice is melting faster than it used to. If substantial melting occurs in Antarctica, rising sea levels could displace millions of people living in coastal communities.

These kinds of changes don't happen overnight, but unfortunately the wheels are already in motion. Scientific evidence points to human activities as the primary driver of modern climate change. On the bright side, indi-

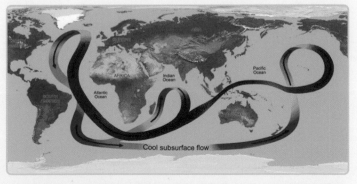

Currents circulate water and nutrients around the globe.

viduals, organizations, companies, and governments can all take steps to reduce their carbon footprints and slow the rate of change going forward.

Three hundred miles away from the Danger Islands, another penguin colony nests within a Marine Protected Area (MPA). Humans are not allowed to fish there, which protects the penguins' food supply. But around the Danger Islands—along the entire Antarctic Peninsula, in fact—no such rules exist.

Should they?

A question of this size is bigger than one scientist.

PROTECTING ANTARCTICA

At the time of the Danger Islands expedition, the only Marine Protected Area in all of Antarctica was a 36,300-square-mile region surrounding the South Orkney Islands. Many scientists and conservationists want to protect more of the Southern Ocean, but decision making in Antarctica is especially complicated. The continent is a vast wilderness without its own government, cities, or full-time human residents. So, policies about what happens in and around Antarctica are set by the countries that conduct scientific research there. And when it comes to conservation priorities, they don't always agree with one another.

Commission members meet annually.

Heather gathers a team. Experts of all sorts, united.
Together they hatch a plan. An expedition. Their goal:
to count and study penguins in the Danger Islands.

From New York, Heather will serve as "mission control,"
monitoring the ever-changing ice conditions from a distance.

In the Falkland Islands, ten scientists board the
Hans Hansson—their
temporary home,
their floating
lab. Their ride
to and from one
of the harshest,
most isolated places
on Earth.

Finally, almost two years after Heather first spotted those pink streaks, they launch.

Next stop: the Danger Islands.

MEET *HANS*

To access the remote Danger Islands, the research team needs a nimble ship that can handle some gnarly weather. *Hans Hansson* has a reinforced steel hull (for the Southern Ocean's icy waters) and is just the right size—small enough to maneuver close to shore, yet large enough to house the research team and crew for an entire month. Their living quarters are cozy—comfortable, but not luxurious. Scientists and crewmembers all dine together and each cabin features an upper and lower berth, like bunk beds.

After a queasy four-day ocean crossing, the air thickens with an unmistakable aroma. Ripe, fishy, and slightly sweet—hello, guano!

Squawking echoes from the shore.

Then, alongside the ship swim the creatures responsible for the noise, the odor, and the giant guano stain that began it all . . .

Adélie penguins! Lots of them.

WHO'S WHO

Penguins are widespread throughout the Southern Hemisphere, but only four out of those seventeen species are year-round residents of Antarctica. Emperor penguins are relatively easy to identify on account of their large size, but Adélie, chinstrap, and gentoo penguins can be harder to tell apart.

PENGUIN	TELL-TALE FEATURES	TYPICAL WEIGHT	TYPICAL HEIGHT
Adélie	Ring of white feathers around each eye	10–11 lb	27 in
Chinstrap	Thin stripe of black feathers under the chin, like the strap to an invisible party hat	10–11 lb	28 in
Gentoo	Flame-orange beak; white patches above eyes; peach-colored feet	11–13 lb	30 in
Emperor	Slender curved beak; golden feathers on the sides of the neck	64–84 lb	44 in

It's December, Antarctica's warmest month, but even now, treacherous sheets of floating ice surround the Danger Islands. Heather transmits fresh satellite photos to the team daily to ensure *Hans* doesn't get iced in. In a region famous for unpredictable conditions, having a "quick getaway" plan is a must.

Each morning, an inflatable boat ferries the scientists and their gear ashore.

THE GEAR

For a typical day of penguin counting, each person carries a handheld clicker, radio, camera, weatherproof paper and pens, binoculars, and a backpack with extra clothes, food, and water. Depending on the day's tasks, they might also bring equipment such as buckets, sample-collection vials, time-lapse cameras, and laptop computers. And on every shore excursion, just in case they get temporarily stranded, the team brings along a survival kit with camping gear and several days' worth of supplies.

Harsh sun radiates overhead. Slick guano lurks underfoot. In Antarctica, proper attire keeps everyone safe, and (usually) out of the muck.

No shortcuts allowed when counting penguins. The total will show how this colony compares to others. How it changes over time.

Ready, set, go! The team lines up and rolls, like a wave, across the island.

Click, click.

Click, click, click.

Tally counters in-hand, they count each zone three times for accuracy. Occupied nests only—penguins out for a waddle don't qualify.

DRESSING FOR SUCCESS

Weather in Antarctica can change in an instant, so scientists grow accustomed to putting on and taking off layers throughout the day. From the inside, heading outward, those layers typically include a wool base layer, down jacket, windbreaker parka and pants, warm hat, gloves, sunglasses, and warm, grippy boots. Sunscreen is also a must—when the sun is out, its reflection off the white ice is intense.

Wait, stop! A summer blizzard whips through. Cold bites. Visibility plummets. It's time to make that quick getaway! With sea ice closing in, *Hans* escapes just in time.

From the safety of a neighboring island group, the scientists wait for conditions to improve. Meanwhile, in New York, Heather strategizes. How can they make the most of this unplanned detour?

In satellite imagery, she spots some guano-stained rocks nearby and sends over the coordinates. Gentoo penguins, the team discovers, are colonizing new territory at the base of a retreating glacier. "Bonus" data like this is worth gathering whenever possible. But just over the horizon, their original counts remain unfinished.

By the time it's safe to return to the Danger Islands, only five days remain before it's time to head home. Faced with enormous uncounted areas, they need eyes in the sky. *Whirrrrr*. A drone photographs the islands from above.

To get the full story, the team also digs through layers of old bone and eggshell fragments to estimate the colony's age. They install cameras that will keep snapping photos for months. And scrape up fresh guano to study its color and contents. The pinker the guano, the more krill the birds have been eating.

The scientists screen wash excavated samples to look for evidence of colonies from long ago.

27

As humans criss-cross the islands counting (and re-counting), penguins come and go. Heading to sea to hunt. Returning to nests, bellies stuffed with krill and fish.

Clamoring. Waddling. Braying hello.
Squabbling over prized nest rocks.

SURVIVAL OF THE FITTEST

It's not unusual for scientists to find different penguin species mingling together because their ranges overlap. But each one thrives under its own set of conditions. Gentoo penguins, for example, are flexible about what they eat, and where and when they reproduce. They are quite adaptable. But Adélie and chinstrap penguins have more rigid habits and adapt slowly. This makes them more vulnerable to environmental changes.

Exhausted, the team members return to the *Hans Hansson*. On deck, they hose off stinky gear. Inside, warm showers await.

In Antarctica, the December sun stays up until midnight. So do many of the scientists. Crunching numbers, making plans, listening to leopard seal calls echo through their cabins until . . . *zzzzzzzz*.

Survey complete, the explorers pack up,
return home, and piece together their
observations. Scientists love a good puzzle.

The team tallies up hand-counted penguins.
Merges drone photos into giant mosaics.
And creates a computer program to count
the photographed nests.

They check the numbers, and check again,
then announce . . .

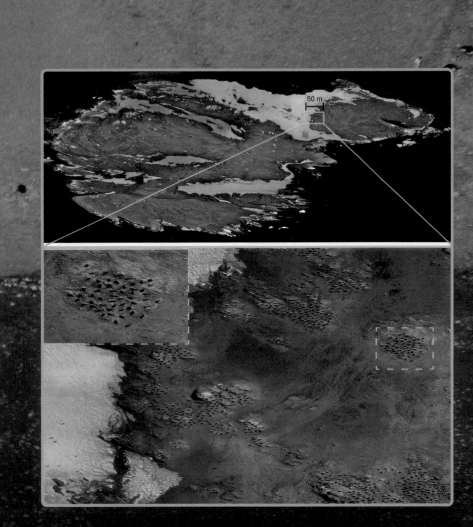

Zooming in on this mosaic of Beagle Island [above] reveals numerous clusters of nesting penguins [below].

1.5 MILLION Adélie penguins are nesting in the Danger Islands!

The population on these nine tiny islands outnumbers the rest of the Antarctic Peninsula's Adélies *combined*.

The news comes just in time. Plans are underway to expand a Marine Protected Area nearby. Heather and her team can now recommend one more addition. . . .

The Danger Islands, off the tip of the Antarctic Peninsula, are teeming with penguins. And now, the whole world knows it.

WHAT'S NEXT?

Fieldwork in Antarctica is hard, and it's not possible to visit every colony every year. So researchers are fine-tuning techniques to monitor penguin colonies' sizes and diets remotely.

From the size of a guano stain in a satellite photo, scientists can calculate a pretty accurate estimate of a colony's size. Especially for Adélies, which nest in a predictable, evenly spaced pattern.

Remember how the expedition team analyzed all that fresh guano? Back at home, they used that information to develop a color-coded key for satellite photos. The pinker

the pixels, the more krill a penguin colony is eating. Whiter pixels mean the birds are eating more fish. Now they can check in from afar, and even look back in time, analyzing older satellite photos to see what the birds were eating decades ago.

The Danger Islands colony used to be even larger. The expedition team reviewed more than thirty years' worth of satellite images and learned it has been shrinking since the late 1990s. But not at the alarming rate seen elsewhere in the Antarctic Peninsula. Why the difference? Could it be the Danger Islands' year-round sea ice? The fact that krill fishing is less common in those waters? It's too soon to know, but with more data, and time to test their hypotheses, scientists hope to find out.

Conservation efforts march (slowly) onward. To expand or establish a new Marine Protected Area (MPA) in the Antarctic region, every single member of the Commission for the Conservation of Antarctic Marine Living Resources (CCAMLR) must agree. Representing governments from around the world, the members don't all see eye to eye. But in 2016, after years of difficult negotiations, the entire Commission—all twenty-four countries, plus the European Union—approved a 600,000-square-mile MPA in the Ross Sea region, making it the world's largest.

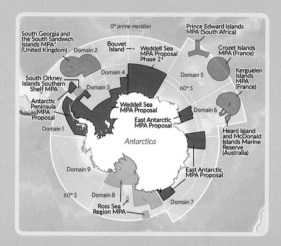

However, as of this writing, the waters around the Danger Islands remain unprotected. Additional MPAs have been proposed in three highly vulnerable areas: East Antarctica, the Weddell Sea, and the Antarctic Peninsula. Most Commission members (all but two) support establishing these new sanctuaries to limit the impact of human activities in the region. But for seven years running, meetings to consider the expansion have ended in stalemates. Until everyone is on board, business continues as usual. Fortunately, so does the research.

The biggest thing we humans can do to protect penguins is take action to slow climate change. Unfortunately, the threats penguins face stand to increase dramatically if we don't change our ways and prioritize our planet's health. But if we *do*—by reducing greenhouse gas emissions, by investing more in "green" technology innovations, by using less stuff—together we could make a meaningful difference. Wildlife around the world would benefit. And so would we.

Become a Citizen Scientist

From anywhere in the world, *you* can contribute to ongoing penguin research! Help spot guano stains in satellite imagery with MAPPPD (the Mapping Application for Penguin Populations and Projected Dynamics) or count penguins in time-lapse photos with Penguin Watch. With a trusted adult, search online for "penguin citizen science" to learn how.

Further Reading

Davies, Nicola and Catherine Rayner (illustrator). *Emperor of the Ice: How a Changing Climate Affects a Penguin Colony*. Candlewick Press, 2023.

Dewey, Jennifer Owings. *Antarctic Journal: Four Months at the Bottom of the World*. Scholastic, 2002.

Gianferrari, Maria and Jieting Chen (illustrator). *Ice Cycle: Poems about the Life of Ice*. Millbrook Press, 2022.

Minoglio, Andrea and Laura Fanelli (illustrator). *Our World Out of Balance: Understanding Climate Change and What We Can Do*. Blue Dot Kids Press, 2021.

Young, Karen Romano and Angela Hsieh (illustrator). *Antarctica: The Melting Continent*. What on Earth Publishing, 2022.

About the Expedition

The Danger Islands expedition took place in December 2015. Research scientists and graduate students at multiple institutions collaborated to plan the project, execute the field surveys, and analyze the satellite and drone images. The team included Alex Borowicz, Gemma Clucas, Steven Forrest, Tom Hart, Rachael Herman, Stéphanie Jenouvrier, Heather J. Lynch, Philip McDowall, Michael J. Polito, Melissa Rider, Thomas Sayre-McCord, Mathew Schwaller, Hanumant Singh, and Casey Youngflesh. The information they gathered and the techniques they developed continue to inform research and conservation policies throughout the Antarctic Peninsula.

Dedication

For science heroes everywhere—past, present, and future—
whose dedication informs and inspires.

About the Author

Helen Taylor is a science-loving children's author whose favorite questions are "how?" and "why?". She started telling quirky stories in the museum world, about polar bear hair plugs, catfish physicals, and other curiosities. Now, she writes books that inspire kids to wonder about their world in new ways. Helen is also the author of *How to Eat in Space*, a Junior Library Guild Gold Standard selection. When she's not reading or writing, she enjoys baking, traveling, and searching for banana slugs in the redwoods near her home in Santa Cruz, California.

HOW NATURE WORKS books don't just catalog the natural world in beautiful photographs. They seek to understand why nature functions as it does. They ask questions, and they encourage readers to ask more. They explore nature's mysteries, sharing what we know and celebrating what we have yet to discover. Other **HOW NATURE WORKS** titles include:

Extreme Survivors:
Animals That Time Forgot
Kimberly Ridley
978-0-88448-743-2

Don't Mess With Me:
The Strange Lives of Venomous Sea Creatures
Paul Erickson
978-0-88448-552-0

**One Iguana,
Two Iguanas:**
A Story of Accident, Natural Selection, and Evolution
Sneed B. Collard III
978-0-88448-650-3

Catching Air:
Taking the Leap with Gliding Animals
Sneed B. Collard III
978-0-88448-883-5